Starting Early

The Ten Steps to Financial Freedom

Starting Early

Early

The Ten Steps to Financial Freedom

A 57-minute guide to building long-term wealth

PIERRE LEVER

T

Troubador Publishing Ltd
Unit E2 Airfield Business Park
Harrison Road, Market Harborough
Leicestershire LE16 7UL
Tel: 0116 279 2299
Email: books@troubador.co.uk
Web: www.troubador.co.uk

ISBN 978 1 83628 044 6

British Library Cataloguing in Publication Data.
A catalogue record for this book is available from the British Library.

Printed and bound in Great Britain by 4edge Limited
Typeset in 11pt Minion Pro by Troubador Publishing Ltd, Leicester, UK

To Sarah, Eleanor, Alice, Kitty (and, of course, Bertie).
Thank you for the love, support, and inspiration.

Contents

Introduction

Practical steps that will be financially life-changing.

Financial freedom is the ability to continue funding the lifestyle you want after you have stopped working, and the goal of this book is to help you take less than an hour learning how to get there. Although it is focused on new earners, it will be valuable to anyone who is unsure what they should do to build long-term wealth.

Financial literacy is rarely covered in depth at school or university. And yet the importance of learning how to achieve financial security is difficult to overstate. This book is intended to fill some of the most important gaps in knowledge.

You will learn when to start investing, how much to set aside, what type of investments to make, the financial pitfalls to avoid, whether and when to buy a home, the key financial incentives that you should pursue, and how to think about career choices.

The ten steps in *Starting Early* represent the consistent habits of ordinary earners who achieve financial freedom, and which you can also adopt. They are the building blocks of wealth that many people later in life wish they had known about early on.

Although it is deliberately short, this is not a get-rich-quick book. In fact, the better mindset over the next ten chapters is that slow and steady wins the race.

In *Everyday Millionaires*,[1] the authors studied the income and spending habits of thousands of people who had obtained financial security. They found that the top three professions to do this were accountants, teachers and engineers, and that 79% achieved their goals by investing money earned from their salaries. In other words, you do not need to be in the top 1% of earners to become financially free, and you can get there without needing an inheritance, or other windfall.

This is the third in the 57 Minute book collection. As with the first two books, it is brief enough to read in under an hour.

- *57 Minutes: All That Stands Between You and a Better Life*,[2] shared insights about finding happiness.

1   Chris Hogan (2019), *Everyday Millionaires: How Ordinary People Built Extraordinary Wealth and How You Can Too*, Ramsay Press, ISBN 9780977489527

2   Mike Jackson and Pierre Lever (2011), *57 Minutes: All That Stands Between You and a Better Life*, ISBN 9781105209079

- *Management in 57 Minutes*,[3] focused on the essence of good leadership for the aspiring manager.

Starting Early will allow you to spend less than an hour of your day learning practical steps that will be financially life-changing.

Let's get started.

---

3   Mike Jackson and Pierre Lever (2015), *Management in 57 Minutes: Leadership Essentials for New Manager*, ISBN 9781508814863

Start Early

Give compound interest time to work its magic.

There is no quick fix to financial freedom. 95% of people who build financial security take more than ten years to do so.[4]

That is why the first, and most important, principle of financial freedom is to start early. And that is because of what is known as the miracle of compound interest.

Compound interest is the process of earning interest on the money you save *and* on the interest itself. If you invest $1,000 and earn a 7% annual return, you will have $1,070 at the end of the year. But at the end of year two, you will have $1,145 rather than $1,140, because the 7% applies to the full $1,070.

Big deal, you may be thinking. An extra $5 barely buys a cup of coffee. But when you watch what compound

---

4   Chris Hogan (2019), *Everyday Millionaires: How Ordinary People Built Extraordinary Wealth and How You Can Too*, Ramsay Press, ISBN 9780977489527

interest does to large numbers, in later years, you start to realise how significant it can be.

Let's take an example. Just before we do, you should note that for this example, and others throughout the book, you will see a figure of 7% as the expected annual return. You may wonder where this number comes from, or whether it is realistic. As we will learn in Chapter 3, it is not only achievable but the minimum that a truly long-term investor should expect.

Jane and Mary are friends who graduate from university together. Both get a job with comparable earning power over the course of their careers.

Jane starts saving $250 a month from her very first salary payment, at the age of twenty-two, and earns a 7% annual return. She never increases her payments beyond $250 a month. She saves for a total of forty years, until she turns sixty-two.

Mary does not see the point of setting money aside at such an early age. $250 pays for a few more nights out each month. Instead, she only starts saving when she is thirty-seven. She invests $500 a month and earns a 7% return. She saves for twenty-five years, until she is also sixty-two.

By this point, Jane, who invested $120,000 over a forty-year period, has a pot of over $660,000. But Mary, who invested $150,000 over twenty-five years, has $407,000.

In short, Jane ends up with 62% *more* than Mary, despite having invested 20% *less*. This is all because Jane started so much earlier and was able to give compound interest time to work its magic.

In fact, had Jane wanted to, she could have withdrawn her money when she was fifty-five, a full seven years before Mary, and still had the same amount that Mary does by the age of sixty-two.

The last few years before you access your funds is when you create the lion's share of your wealth, through the effect of compound interest. The earlier you start, the larger the pot of money for compound interest to work its magic on, and especially in those crucial few years before you decide to down tools.

In Jane's case, $192,000, or 29% of her overall pot, was from compound interest earned purely in the last five years before she took out her money.

Much of the personal finance literature obsesses about finding the highest rates of return. And, of course, the rate of return is important. But investing early is more important. It is also easier. Starting early is within your control. Trying to find outsized market returns is not.

To have matched Jane's pot of money, Mary would have had to find consistent returns of 10% a year, versus Jane's 7%. Or, she could have just started saving when she was twenty-two, not thirty-seven.

The table below gives a more detailed view of the effects of compound interest based on the starting age for investing. It shows how a monthly savings amount, earning 7% interest annually, translates into a total pot of money by the age of sixty-two, depending on when someone starts to invest.

Total achieved at 62, with a 7% annual return, and for someone starting to invest at the following age:

Monthly savings	Age 42	Age 32	Age 22
$100	$52,397	$122,709	$264,012
$250	$130,991	$306,772	$660,031
$500	$261,983	$613,544	$1,320,062
$1,000	$523,965	$1,227,087	$2,640,125
$1,500	$785,948	$1,840,631	$3,960,187
$2,000	$1,047,931	$2,454,175	$5,280,250

Invest early, be patient and watch compound interest do the hard work, for you.

Key Message
Begin investing as early as you can so that, over time, compound interest can create a life-changing effect on your wealth.

Stick to a Budget

The best predictor of wealth is how much you save,
rather than how much you earn.

Living within your means is important for two reasons: you will not need to take on debt and it permits you to set aside savings that you can then invest.

94% of ordinary earners that achieve financial security keep their spending below their income.[5]

The best predictor of wealth is how much you save rather than how much you earn. That is why, of all the topics discussed in this book, one of the most important is your ability to create savings each month, to invest over the long-term.

This is an easy message to write but a challenging thing to do. It requires some sacrifice. But there are some

---

5   Chris Hogan (2019), *Everyday Millionaires: How Ordinary People Built Extraordinary Wealth and How You Can Too*, Ramsay Press, ISBN 9780977489527

tried-and-tested concepts to keep in mind, which will help you.

Track Your Spending

This does not have to be a sophisticated exercise. You can just use a simple Excel spreadsheet and list out the different items of expenses you have every month. Or you can download one of the many spending and budgeting apps that give a single view of all your spending in one place.

However you do it, you need to track where your money is going each month. Otherwise, you are flying blind.

Create a Budget That Allows You to Save

This is the part of financial freedom planning that new earners struggle with the most.

If you are living independently, you will have essentials such as rent, groceries, transport and utility bills that you need to pay for each month.

You will also want to keep money aside for nights out with friends, to fund at least one holiday a year and other nice things. Life is there to be enjoyed, not just observed.

Once all of this is paid for, the remainder needs to be set aside as savings, to invest. But, if you find that you do not have *any* money left over to save, you will need to re-examine how much of your spending you can reduce.

To coin a phrase from Morgan Housel, the author of *The Psychology of Money*,[6] savings simply represent the gap between your income and your ego. You should review how many of those nice things your ego demands, and how many you can trade off. If you are truly intent on reaching a point of financial freedom, there is no alternative. Or, to put it another way, making 0% savings will result in close to 0% chance of achieving financial freedom.

Ditch Credit Cards

Credit cards allow you to spend a bank's money and then pay them back at the end of the month. Credit cards make it all too easy to spend that little bit extra here and there, because you do not immediately see the money coming out of your own account.

Credit cards discourage self-control and banks know this. Banks expect you to occasionally spend so much in a month that you will be unable to pay back the money on time at the end of the month. That is when they start charging you debt interest. Eye-wateringly high levels of interest.

---

6   Morgan Housel (2020), *The Psychology of Money, Timeless Lessons on Wealth, Greed, and Happiness*, Harriman House, ISBN 9780857197689

At the time of writing, the median interest rate for credit cards was 24.37%.[7]

There is another, pernicious, side effect of late payment.

When you fail to make payments on time, it can affect your credit score. A credit score is something that mortgage lenders look at to ensure that you have a good history of paying off bills. A good credit score can be built by making repayments on time and using up as little of your available credit as possible. But if your credit score is poor, you might only be able to secure a mortgage with more expensive repayment terms.

Given that a home is normally the most expensive asset you will ever own, bad terms on a mortgage can really eat into your savings.

When you are starting out with your first job, skip credit cards. Use debit cards instead, as these take money directly from your account and avoid you falling into a credit card debt trap.

Cancel Unused Subscriptions

The average consumer spends $219[8] a month on subscriptions to digital content, gyms and other services

---

7   https://www.investopedia.com/articles/01/061301. asp#:~:text=Most%20credit%20cards%20have%20 variable,in%20Investopedia's%20database%20was%2024.37%25

8   https://www.cnbc.com/2022/06/02/consumers-spend-133-more-monthly-on-subscriptions-than-they-realize.html

but, when prompted, 42%[9] find subscriptions they no longer use but are still paying for. And almost a third of subscribers[10] dip into savings or borrow money to fund these.

Make sure you are not one of them. Keep a tally of your own subscriptions and cancel the ones you do not see any benefit from or rarely use. The modest savings from each cancelled subscription can amount to a significant sum over time.

Double check each line item from your bank statement as well as the subscriptions setting on your phone, where digital subscriptions increasingly appear, and keep a close eye out for those unwanted subscriptions each month.

Avoid Expensive Cars

A nice car is something many new earners want to buy, either as a status symbol or for the feel-good effect of material wealth. Avoiding this temptation is one of the best things you can do to ensure you keep your spending below your income.

Typically, a new car loses over 50% of its value in the first three years. And many car owners take on a loan to

9   https://www.cnbc.com/2022/06/02/consumers-spend-133-more-monthly-on-subscriptions-than-they-realize.html

10   https://kpmg.com/uk/en/home/media/press-releases/2022/07/a-third-of-consumers-use-savings-to-cover-the-costs-of-media-subscriptions.html

buy a car which they then must pay back, with elevated levels of interest. This makes car ownership one of the worst uses of spare income.

For example, if you buy a new car for $25,000, the chances are that three years later the car can only be sold for around $10,000. If you have taken out a full loan, this is likely to come to over $30,000, including interest, that will need to be paid back, meaning you have lost $20,000 in three years.

This is why car loans are 'bad' compared to, say, a 'good' loan or mortgage, for a home. Car loans are high-interest products for a depreciating asset. Mortgages are low-interest loans for a, typically, appreciating one. More on this later.

To recap: track your spending, set a budget, avoid credit cards and nice cars, cancel unwanted subscriptions and do what you need to set aside money to invest.

Let's now get into the substance of what you should invest *in* to get the best bang for your buck.

Key Message
Track your spending, set a budget, and avoid credit cards, nice cars, and unnecessary subscriptions, so that you always have savings left over to invest.

Buy Index Funds

Buy the haystack, not the needle.

There is a bewildering array of investment vehicles to choose from. You can invest in interest-earning cash accounts, or individual stocks, or managed funds, or many other options. The market is steered by a financial services industry that has become masterful in its approach to encouraging you to choose their products.

But as a first-time earner looking to make a long-term investment decision, the question is: what is the best option for you?

Decades of research on this topic has produced a clear answer. The best way to grow your wealth over the long-term is to invest in a diversified range of stocks, which make up a large market index. And the best way to do this is through what are known as index funds.

Index funds do not try and beat the market. Instead, they buy stocks of every firm listed on it, to match the overall performance. So, when you invest in an index fund, you diversify your investment across every stock listed on the index that the fund is tracking. In other words, you buy the haystack, not the needle.

For one hundred years, the S&P 500, which tracks the performance of the largest five hundred public stocks in the US, has delivered the most reliable, long-term returns of any major index.

Before we look at data about the S&P 500, there is one unavoidable fact related to investing that needs to be understood. It is not possible to generate good returns over the long run without accepting that your investments will drop, sometimes very significantly, at certain periods of time over that long run. And it is impossible to predict when.

In 2022, the S&P 500 fell 19.4%.

In 2002 and 2008, it fell even further.

And on October 19 1987, it lost over 20% of its value in a day.

If you had read this book shortly before any of these dates and subsequently invested in the S&P 500, you would be cursing my name and throwing the book away. But if you had just looked away during any of these moments and continued patiently investing, you would have been richly rewarded over time.

Having a long-term horizon means that it *does not matter* if the market occasionally dips, or even crashes. Unlike your odds when you visit a casino, your chances of seeing positive results from the S&P 500 increase the *longer* you invest.

In the last one hundred years, there is no single twenty-year period that saw negative returns in the S&P 500. Even the worst twenty-year period generated annual returns of 1.90%, and the best returned 18.30%. And if you expand your view out to look at each thirty-year period, the worst of these gave annual returns of 7.80%.

If you want to see compound interest working its magic on your hard-earned savings over extended periods of time, investing in an S&P 500 index fund is as sensible a choice as you could make.

Warren Buffett is recognised as one of the world's most successful ever investors. He is worth over $120 billion and built his wealth by actively selecting and holding stocks in companies which he believed were fantastic long-term businesses.

If you have the skill and patience to do what Warren does, great. But for the 99.99% of us that do not have these attributes (and for 100% of first-time earners), the best thing you can do is to begin your long-term investing by using the S&P 500.

Even Warren Buffett himself has said that, when he dies, he wants the bulk of his estate to be invested in index funds.[11] If it is good enough for Warren, it should be good enough for us.

If using an S&P 500 index fund is the most sensible long-term investment for the first-time earner, which fund provider should you choose?

> ### *Key Message*
> *Invest in a fund that tracks a major index like the S&P 500, so you create diversification, rather than trying to rely on the fortunes of a handful of individual stocks.*

11   https://www.cnbc.com/2019/02/26/warren-buffett-wants-90-percent-of-his-estate-invested-in-index-funds.html

Beware High Fees

*Low-cost funds make you
disproportionately wealthier.*

The stock market is highly efficient. Stock prices typically reflect information that all investors have access to, and so it becomes extremely difficult to find a stock about which you know something that others do not. It is what is known as the 'efficient market hypothesis'. It is one of the reasons that individual stock picking is so hard to succeed at over the long-term.

This is why, in the previous chapter, we explained that it is better to use index funds, as these help you naturally diversify your investments across a large market index, and avoid you being a hostage to the fortunes of a small handful of stocks you have tried to select.

In the case of the S&P 500, all index fund providers buy the largest five hundred public stocks on the US market. There may be small differences in their methodologies but, over time, there will be little difference in their overall performance.

If that is the case, how do you know which fund provider to choose?

The answer is: the one with the *lowest fees*.

Morningstar, a financial services research firm, studied the variables that best predict the success of a fund.[12] They discovered that the most predictive variable is not performance but cost, and that the cheapest 20% of funds were three times as likely to do well than the most expensive 20%.

Some funds are managed by fund managers. These are actively managed funds. The fees involved for these are higher because they are used to pay for expensive salaries. There is little point in choosing an actively managed fund because fund managers tend not to outperform passive index funds,[13] which are much lower cost.

Some of the lowest-cost type of index funds are called Exchange Traded Funds, or ETFs. These are funds that trade on stock markets and simulate a basket of stocks that track an index, such as the S&P 500.

The cheapest S&P 500 ETFs are often run by larger financial services firms, like Vanguard, Fidelity, State

---

12 https://www.morningstar.co.uk/uk/news/149421/how-fund-fees-are-the-best-predictor-of-returns.aspx

13 S&P Dow Jones indices SPIVS study (2022), https://www.spglobal.com/spdji/en/research-insights/spiva/

Street and BlackRock.[14] This is because they have a large volume of investors which, in turn, allows them to keep their fees down. For the avoidance of doubt, this is not a promotion for those brands. There are many large firms you can choose from. The point is simply that low cost does not have to mean low quality. You can have the benefit of choosing a provider that is reputable *and* cheap.

Let's demonstrate how low-cost funds make you disproportionately wealthier.

At the time of writing, one of the most expensive and actively managed funds charges 1.07% in annual fees. One of the cheapest passive funds charges 0.07%.

On the face of it, this may seem insignificant. 1.07% is only 1% higher than the alternative, and 1% seems like a small number. But in terms of the impact on your money, the cumulative effect of this extra 1% over time is enormous.

Let's imagine this time that both Mary and Jane start investing $250 a month, aged twenty-two, and earn 7% interest a year. They leave their money to grow until they are sixty-two. The only difference this time is the fund provider they choose.

Mary chooses the 1.07% fund, run by a company with a website describing the impressive pedigree of its fund managers.

14   https://www.investopedia.com/investing/top-sp-500-etfs/

Jane chooses a fund provider highlighting its 0.07% fee prominently on its website.

What happens?

Jane ends up with an amount, after fees, of $647,000. But Mary has $490,000, which is $157,000, or 24%, less than Jane. And all because of the 1% difference in fees.

There was once a well-known commercial for a beer called Stella Artois. It had the tag line 'reassuringly expensive'. In other words, you get what you pay for. The opposite is true for index tracking funds. Choose 'reassuringly cheap' and you will end up wealthier.

Now we know how important it is to start investing early and to choose a low-cost S&P 500 index fund, the next question is: how much should you invest at the beginning?

Key Message
Always choose index funds with the lowest annual fees.

Begin Small
(But Begin)

Don't let the perfect be the enemy of the good.

We have already seen that $250 a month, saved over forty years and with a 7% return, provided Jane with a pot of just over $660,000 by the age of sixty-two. We also detailed what would happen if she invested higher amounts at different starting points in her life.

But if Jane is on a salary of $38,000, the average graduate starting salary at the time of writing, it may be difficult for her to contemplate $250 a month, even if she does all that she can to stick to a budget.

Jane might then be tempted to delay investing until her salary starts to grow. This would be a mistake. Instead, Jane can invest a *small percentage* of her salary, rather than a large, fixed amount, and gradually increase the percentage figure each year.

This stepping-up approach is always better than putting off the start of your investing journey.

Procrastination is the enemy of financial freedom, so don't let the perfect be the enemy of the good.

Assume that Jane follows this approach and starts by investing just 3% of her income each month. This would represent $100 a month.

She then increases her savings rate by 1% of her income a year, until she reaches 15% of her income being saved each month.

This means that at the age of twenty-three, she is investing 4% of her income, at the age of twenty-four she is investing 5%, and so on. When Jane is thirty-four, she freezes the savings percentage at 15% of her income and continues to invest 15% for the next twenty-eight years, until she turns sixty-two.

To make the scenario even more realistic, let's also factor in the likely effect from salary growth that Jane might hope to achieve through pay rises and job moves. This could amount to at least a 3% salary increase each year, over the course of her career.

In this scenario, by the time she is sixty-two, Jane will have a pot of over $1.4 million.

This compares to the $660,000 she had by investing a fixed sum of $250 a month, in the Chapter 1 illustration, or to the $407,000 Mary achieved by delaying until she was thirty-seven and investing $500 a month.

Just to be clear, if you can invest a large percentage of your income each month from the get-go, that's great.

It is obvious that the more you save from day one, the better. But if this is unaffordable, as it is likely to be for many people reading this book, you must avoid delaying your investing journey. It is OK, instead, to begin small, so long as you do begin.

The next important question to address, is how to go about timing your investments. There is clear evidence about the best way to do this, so let's take a look.

> ### Key Message
> It is better to begin investing a small percentage of your income, than to delay until you can afford a larger starting amount.

Dollar Cost Average

Trying to time the market is a fool's errand.

In Chapter 2, we talked about the importance of saving money from your salary, to invest. But how often should you invest your savings into an index fund? Should you build up a lump sum and only make the occasional investment when you think the market is dipping? And if so, how do you know when to catch the lows?

Predicting market dips is impossible to do consistently. Trying to time the market is a fool's errand.

Instead, the more reliable approach is known as dollar cost averaging. This involves investing the same amount of money, at regular intervals, over a prolonged period.

Dollar cost averaging allows you to lower your average cost over the long run and reduce the impact of big market swings or volatility. Let's take an example.

Say Mary keeps aside $3,000 over the course of a year and then decides to invest in an S&P 500 ETF in one lump sum. She buys fifty-five shares in December. The cost per share is $54.54.

Jane, on the other hand, sets up a monthly instalment plan with her S&P 500 ETF provider for $250 per month, starting in January of that year. By December, she too has invested $3,000.

In total, Jane ends up with fifty-eight shares, meaning her average cost per share was $51.72, or almost $3 less per share than Mary.

It was impossible for Jane to know which months the cost of the ETF shares would be higher or lower. But with dollar cost averaging, timing is removed from the equation. Dollar cost averaging helps people who do not have large sums to invest in one go reduce their risk over the long run.[15]

There might be times when Mary's lump sum approach would work better. And there is some research suggesting that if you have a very large sum to invest in one go, it might be a superior way to buy into the market.[16] But the reality, for most people reading this book, is that you will lose more than you gain if you try and use the lump sum approach.

To quote Morgan Housel once more: *Dollar cost*

15   E. Napoletano and Benjamin Curry, How To Invest With Dollar Cost Averaging, *Forbes* Mar 21 2023

16   Richard E Williams Ph. D and Peter W Bacon, DBA, CFP (2004), Lump Sum Beats Dollar Cost Averaging: *Journal of Financial Planning*, Vol 17 issue 6

average for life and you'll beat almost everyone who doesn't.[17]

As well as avoiding the pitfalls of market timing, there are other benefits to dollar cost averaging.

As it occurs automatically, it does not require any effort on your behalf and there is no self-discipline involved. You simply set up a regular monthly payment into your index fund and then just get on with your life.

It also allows you to keep your investing rational. Setting up an automated investment plan means that you eliminate the heat-of-the-moment decisions that normally accompany an effort to time the market, and which rarely end well. It also helps you avoid diverting spare cash towards short-term opportunities. Let's explore why these are usually a bad idea.

> **Key Message**
> Do not try and time the market, just drip feed your savings into an index fund every month and then look away.

---

17 Morgan Housel (2017), @morganhousel on X, 12 April 2017, 4:08pm

Avoid Short-Termism

Quick fixes will slow you down.

When it comes to planning for financial freedom, we have already seen that starting early and investing consistently in index funds over the long-term are key ingredients to success.

Yet, one of the most common pitfalls we encounter, as we progress through our career and gradually earn more money, is the opportunity to make a quick buck.

We may have a friend who convinces us to invest in a sure-fire stock they made money from. There might be an article we come across flagging the next big technology trend, with a list of companies to invest in. Or we might hear coffee-machine chat about a colleague who made a small fortune from bitcoin.

These opportunities can seem highly compelling because they involve a powerful cocktail of a fear of missing out, a quick dopamine hit and the potential of a windfall profit. But, ultimately, these quick fixes will slow you down.

Short-term investing is exciting, long-term index funds are boring. When it comes to achieving financial freedom, choose boring.

The reason for this is simple. It is impossible to know *which* short-term opportunities will succeed. You might occasionally strike gold but if you think you can do this consistently, you are overestimating your skill and underestimating your luck.

Short-term opportunities should be avoided because:

1. *You are likely to lose your money.* Numerous studies point to the fact that 90% of people who trade individual stocks lose money.[18]

2. *You might lose twice over.* The $5,000 you put into an individual stock could have gone into an S&P 500 index fund instead. This means that if your investment did not pay off, you not only fail to gain from that investment, but you have also created an opportunity cost of an extra $5,000 slice of the S&P 500.

18 Bob Pisano (2020), Stock Picking Has a Terrible Track Record, https://www.cnbc.com/2020/09/18/stock-picking-has-a-terrible-track-record-and-its-getting-worse.html

3. *Persistent short-term investing is gambling.* If you are unlucky and lose money the first few times you try, you might assume the odds are in your favour to get lucky the next time. This is known as the gambler's fallacy. It is a fallacy because losing several times does *not* mean you are due a payoff the next time. Conversely, if you score win after win, you might start to believe you have the Midas touch. You will soon discover you do not. In either scenario, you have turned from an investor into a gambler.

4. *You might already own 'the next big thing' through your S&P 500 index fund.* If an innovative technology is being publicised as the boom market of the future, you might be tempted to start picking stocks in that space. But the chances are that your fund will eventually own shares in the best public companies in those markets anyway, because the best companies will gradually find their way into the S&P 500, and then into your index fund.

At this point in the book, with the relentless encouragement to invest in long-term index funds, you might be starting to ask whether there are *any* other investments at all you should consider diversifying with?

The answer to this is yes: your first home.

Invest in a Home

Make yourself wealthier, instead of your landlord.

It is important to understand the difference between good and bad debt, and how this relates to home ownership.

When you start your career, unless you are lucky enough to have a family that can afford to support you, there is a high chance you will be paying rent to a landlord. And rental payments can consume a large chunk of your income each month.

Getting your foot on the property ladder as early as possible is an important component of setting yourself up for financial freedom. It avoids you paying rent and means the money can be used to create ownership in your own home instead.

Doing this is likely to involve you taking on debt in the form of a mortgage. A mortgage is simply a legal charge that a lender has over your property, in exchange for lending you money to buy it.

Although many forms of debt should be avoided, mortgages are a form of debt that can be considered, relatively speaking, good. What do we mean by this?

In Chapter 2, we referred to car loans as bad. This is because a loan to buy a car carries high interest and will eventually leave you with an asset, the car, which is worth less than when you first bought it.

Other forms of bad debt include credit cards, high-interest bank overdrafts and short-term loans from specialist lenders, who sometimes use aggressive loan-recovery techniques.

A loan for a home, on the other hand, is good debt in the sense that mortgages come with *lower* interest than most loans and will leave you with an asset, your home, which is typically *worth more*, over the long-term, than when you first bought it.

A mortgage can also contribute to your pursuit of financial freedom because of the effect of leverage. A mortgage allows you to, in effect, amplify your investment, whilst freeing up more of your own money to put into other investments, like your S&P 500 ETF.

To take a simple example of leverage at work, let's say you put a $20,000 deposit down on a $200,000 home and borrow $180,000 from a bank at a fixed 4.5% annual interest, repayable over twenty-five years. Let's also assume that your home increases in value at 5% a year. After ten years, when you decide to sell up and move, it is worth almost $326,000.

Over the ten years, you will have paid the lender $71,000 in interest as well as then needing to repay the original $180,000. In total, you have paid back $251,000. You are left with $75,000 of value, or equity, in the home, of which $20,000 was your original deposit. This means you have made a profit of $55,000, representing a return of 275% on the original $20,000.

Now let's assume you were able to buy the property in cash for $200,000. Again, it is worth $326,000 after ten years. But this time the profit of $126,000 represents a 63% return on your $200,000.

In scenario one, with a mortgage, you enjoyed a 275% return and in scenario two, without a mortgage, a 63% return. This is leverage at work. In scenario one, less of your own money was needed to own the asset because the bank provided the bulk of the purchase price.

Just to be clear, this is not an advert for mortgage debt. There are pitfalls to taking out a mortgage, including the risk of unaffordable levels of interest and the possibility of the house being worth less when you sell it. Housing normally increases in value but there have been many instances in history of this not being the case, most notably the 2008 sub-prime mortgage crisis which triggered a collapse in global financial markcts.

The point is simply that with a reasonable mortgage, at levels of interest that fall below the likely long-term increase in your property value, you can end up becoming a full property owner whilst also benefiting from the leverage effect of the loan. You will make yourself wealthier, rather than your landlord. And without needing to disrupt the monthly payments into your index fund.

In short, avoid credit cards, car loans and specialist loans but take on a sensible mortgage as quickly as you can afford it, to buy your first home.

Key Message

Focus on buying a home as soon as you can, using an affordable mortgage to get yourself on the housing ladder.

Follow the Incentives

Say yes to a free lunch.

The steps we have described so far make up the core habits of ordinary earners who achieve financial freedom. But there is one other important trait that they have, and which we should explore here.

They use financial incentives in the form of *tax-free wrappers*, *employer contributions*, and *company share schemes*.

The specifics of these incentives vary by country and by employer, but what they have in common is the objective of encouraging you to invest in long-term opportunities.

To accomplish this, they offer tangible benefits to accelerate your own financial journey, and for no additional cost. All you need to do in return is take advantage of them.

In effect, they amount to a free lunch, and you should always try and say yes to a free lunch.

Put Your Index Fund into a Tax-Free Wrapper

When you set up your index fund, there is usually a tax-free wrapper available for you to set the fund up within. These wrappers will be visible through your financial provider's set-up process.

By using a tax-free wrapper – for instance, a Roth IRA in the US or an ISA in the UK – you will pay *no* tax on the long-term growth in your fund. This will have a significant impact on your eventual wealth.

In our example from Chapter 1, in which Jane invested $120,000 over forty years and ended up with a $660,000 pot of money, she would have saved up to $228,000 in taxes, just by putting the index fund within a Roth IRA.

Make sure you use up your full tax-free allowance before you contemplate investing money in funds that will eventually be taxable.

Take Advantage of Employer Contributions

Depending on the industry, many employees will be offered employer contributions to a retirement account – for instance, a 401K in the US, or an employer-backed pension in the UK. And you can normally select an index fund for these contributions to be allocated to.

Often, your employer will agree to match your own contributions, up to a certain limit. This means that if you personally contribute $250 a month into the fund, your employer will turn that in to $500. There are also tax advantages associated with your individual contributions. Your employer can feed the contributions out of your salary *before* income tax is applied, representing a significant tax saving.

There is no good reason to refuse to receive free money from your employer, or tax breaks on your own contributions.

Say Yes to Company Share Schemes

Some employers will offer you the opportunity to participate in their share scheme. These might be in the form of discounted share purchases or share option schemes that allow you to convert options into shares at a reduced price.

Let's say that you are offered 1,500 share options, at what is known as a strike price of $5 per share, and which vest over three years. This would mean that after year three, all 1,500 options will have vested, or become usable. You can then convert the options in to shares, or exercise them, at the $5 strike price.

At this point, if the company share price has reached $15 a share, you can sell the 1,500 shares and make a profit of $10 per share, or $15,000 in total. Alternatively, if the price has dropped, you can choose not to exercise the option at all, meaning you lose nothing. That is why options are valuable. You can choose to use them and make a profit, or to leave them unconverted and lose nothing.

As clear as this may seem, many people do not appreciate the potential benefit of these types of share schemes, due to a lack of understanding of their potential value, or through a sense of trepidation about dealing in options and shares. Do not make the same mistake. If you have an opportunity to participate in your company share scheme, use it.

As we near the end of the book, we will tackle one last question that many people struggle with, and which cuts across several of the topics we have explored so far: how to choose a career path.

> ### Key Message
> *Take advantage of tax-free wrappers, employer contributions, and company share schemes, to accelerate your journey to wealth.*

Pursue Your Talent, Not Just Your Passion

Find your Ikigai

The intention in this book has been to guide you on the path to financial freedom, rather than towards a specific career. As we have already noted, you do not need to be a top earner to eventually achieve a salary-free lifestyle.

Nonetheless, this concluding chapter is about career choices. And that is because it is helpful, especially for aspiring earners, to think in practical terms about choosing a profession. A person trying to figure out what career they may be interested in is often told to pursue their passion. This is, at best, simplistic.

You may have many passions, but you do not need to build a decades-long career around these alone. You can choose a career path that not only matches your interests but also your talents, whilst offering sufficient financial reward to support your lifestyle and to plan for financial freedom. These goals do not have to be mutually exclusive.

Bear in mind that less than half of graduates choose a career that relates to their degree. And many people who choose a specific vocation early in life make a switch later. The idea of the professional pivot is increasingly common, and this can be a healthy thing, so long as you find the right fit each time.

The best framework I have seen for thinking about career fit, is the Japanese concept of *Ikigai*.

In traditional Japanese philosophy, *Ikigai* is about finding your reason for being, '*iki*' meaning life and '*gai*' meaning worth. It has since been adapted[19] to reflect the pursuit of a career which will help you be happy and prosperous.

Ikigai requires you to contemplate four questions. What do you love doing? What are you good at? What can you be paid for? And what does the world need?

If you find a role that enables you to do what you *love*, that you are *good at*, that you can be *paid for*, and that *the world needs*, you have found your *Ikigai*.

But if you ignore some of these points, it can cause career malaise.

Someone who focuses on a role they think they can be good at, and which pays well, but which they have no

---

19   Marc Winn (2014), 'What is your Ikigai?', https://theviewinside. me/what-is-your-ikigai/

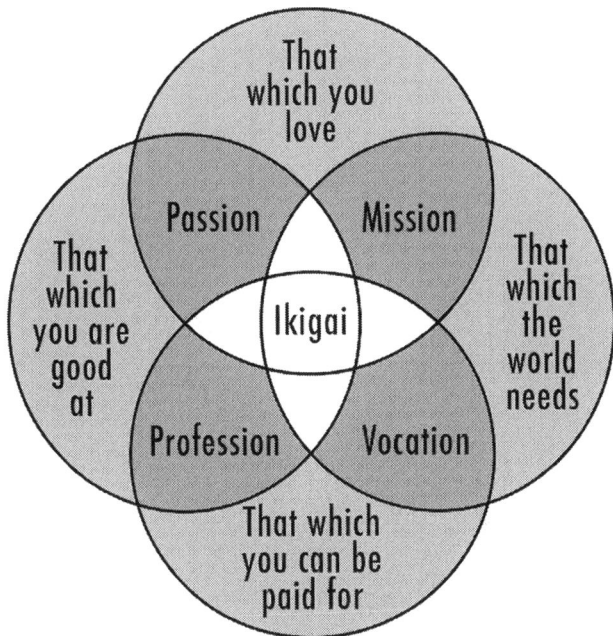

real interest in, may be financially comfortable but feel frustrated.

And someone who finds something they love, are good at and that they can be well paid for, will feel a high level of satisfaction for a while, but if there is no long-term need for the role, or it is in a dying industry, a sense of uselessness will eventually settle in.

Or someone who finds what they love and that the world needs, but which pays a minimal salary, may be fulfilled, which is wonderful, but will struggle to achieve wealth.

There are subtle trade-offs within each of these areas of enquiry. But, as a starting point, *Ikigai* provides both a practical and profound way to think about your future.

It opens your mind to possibilities that may be excluded by just focusing on your passion. Some industries may seem prosaic, or unrelated to your passion, but offer roles *within them* that provide abundant fulfilment and financial reward. As Daniel Pink writes in *Drive*,[20] you can feel tremendous motivation in any role that provides a degree of autonomy, the opportunity to master a skill and a sense of purpose.

When someone asks me for career advice, I begin by asking them to think more about what they want to *do* than what they want to *be*. This is consistent with trying to find your *Ikigai*.

Too often, a person setting out on a new career seeks out a recognisable title without thinking through the day-to-day implications of the responsibilities the role entails.

For example, it may feel good to say: 'I want to be an entrepreneur'. Many people are enthusiastic about starting their own business, in pursuit of the recognition of being a successful start-up founder and having a

---

20 Daniel Pink (2011), *Drive: The Surprising Truth About What Motivates Us*, Canongate Books, ISBN 978-1847677693

celebrated impact in the world. But they frequently then discover that their initial perception of *being* an entrepreneur does not match up to the reality, or *doing*, of entrepreneurship: the long hours, the stress of managing cash flow and raising funds, and the constant need to market their business to others. It is not for everyone.

It is great to seek out roles that excite you and which seem consistent with a passion. And it is understandable to want to have recognition. But it is just as important to think about your talents, both the ones you have and the ones that you want to build upon.

What roles require, and allow you to develop, these skills in a profession that you can have an impact in and for a healthy financial reward?

Once you adopt this type of *Ikigai* mindset, you will find that well-paying, highly satisfying career choices present themselves that might otherwise have been missed.

Key Message
Find a role that allows you to do what you love, are good at, that the world needs, and which funds your savings.

Conclusion:
The Ten Steps to
Financial Freedom

Over the last ten chapters, we have learnt that the secret to building long-term wealth is to spend less than you earn and to invest your savings early and consistently, through dollar cost averaging, into low-cost index funds. We also know that you can start slowly and then step up your savings, why short-termism is your enemy, how mortgage debt can be an effective way to buy a first home, and the importance of tax, and employer, incentives.

Even though the book is deliberately short, it is likely that some of the highlights will gradually slip out of your memory. With that in mind, here is a cheat sheet you can refer to whenever you are making a financial decision.

If you follow these ten steps, you can feel confident that you are on the path to financial freedom.

1. **Start early** – Begin investing as early as you can so that, over time, compound interest can create a life-changing effect on your wealth.

2. **Stick to a budget** – Track your spending, set a budget, and avoid credit cards, nice cars and unnecessary subscriptions, so that you always have savings left over to invest.

3. **Buy index funds** – Invest in a fund that tracks a major index like the S&P 500, so you create diversification, rather than trying to rely on the fortunes of a handful of individual stocks.

4. **Beware high fees** – Always choose index funds with the lowest annual fees.

5. **Begin small (but begin)** – It is better to begin investing a small percentage of your income than to delay until you can afford a larger starting amount.

6. **Dollar cost average** – Do not try and time the market, just drip feed your savings into an index fund every month and then look away.

7. **Avoid short-termism** – Ignore short-term opportunities as, over the long run, you will lose

money and become a gambler rather than an investor.

8. **Invest in a home** – Focus on buying a home as soon as you can, using an affordable mortgage to get yourself on the housing ladder.

9. **Follow the incentives** – Take advantage of tax-free wrappers, employer contributions and company share schemes to accelerate your journey to wealth.

10. **Pursue your talent, not just your passion** – Find a role that allows you to do what you love, are good at, that the world needs and which funds your savings.

Recommended Reading List

If you want to invest more time to delve into the topics covered in this book, you should buy some, or all, of the following:

Everyday Millionaires, Chris Hogan
What They Don't Teach You About Money, Claer Barrett
The Algebra of Wealth, Scott Galloway
The Psychology of Money, Morgan Housel
Invest your Way to Financial Freedom, Ben Carlson & Robin Powell
The Barefoot Investor, Scott Pape
Smart Money, Smart Kids, Rachel Cruze and Dave Ramsey

Acknowledgements

I would like to thank the following people who helped in reviewing, or inspiring, much of the content of *Starting Early*: Hamid Abassalty, Eleanor Lever, Emily Pickup, Kitty Lever, Alice Lever, Sarah Lever, and with particular thanks to Dan Brereton for his feedback and detailed analysis of the financial projections.

About the Author

Pierre Lever is a start-up investor and author. Pierre sits on the board of several UK-based companies and is co-author, with Mike Jackson, of the 57 Minute book series, popular short-format guides about life, leadership and, with this most recent addition, money.

Over the past thirty years, Pierre has lived and worked in cities across Europe and Asia and has become an avid student of human behaviour. Throughout his career as a lawyer, business leader and investor, he has subscribed to the view that to live is to learn.

Pierre lives in the UK with his wife Sarah, and together they have three children, Eleanor, Alice and Kitty.

This book is printed on paper from sustainable sources managed under the Forest Stewardship Council (FSC) scheme.

It has been printed in the UK to reduce transportation miles and their impact upon the environment.

For every new title that Troubador publishes, we plant a tree to offset CO_2, partnering with the More Trees scheme.

MORE TREES
LET'S PLANT A BILLION TREES

For more about how Troubador offsets its environmental impact, see www.troubador.co.uk/sustainability-and-community